A Sad Girls Poetry

Olivia Schwab-Vidal

Presentation by *BookLeaf Publishing*

Web: www.bookleafpub.com

E-mail: info@bookleafpub.com

ISBN: 9789357740142

First edition 2023

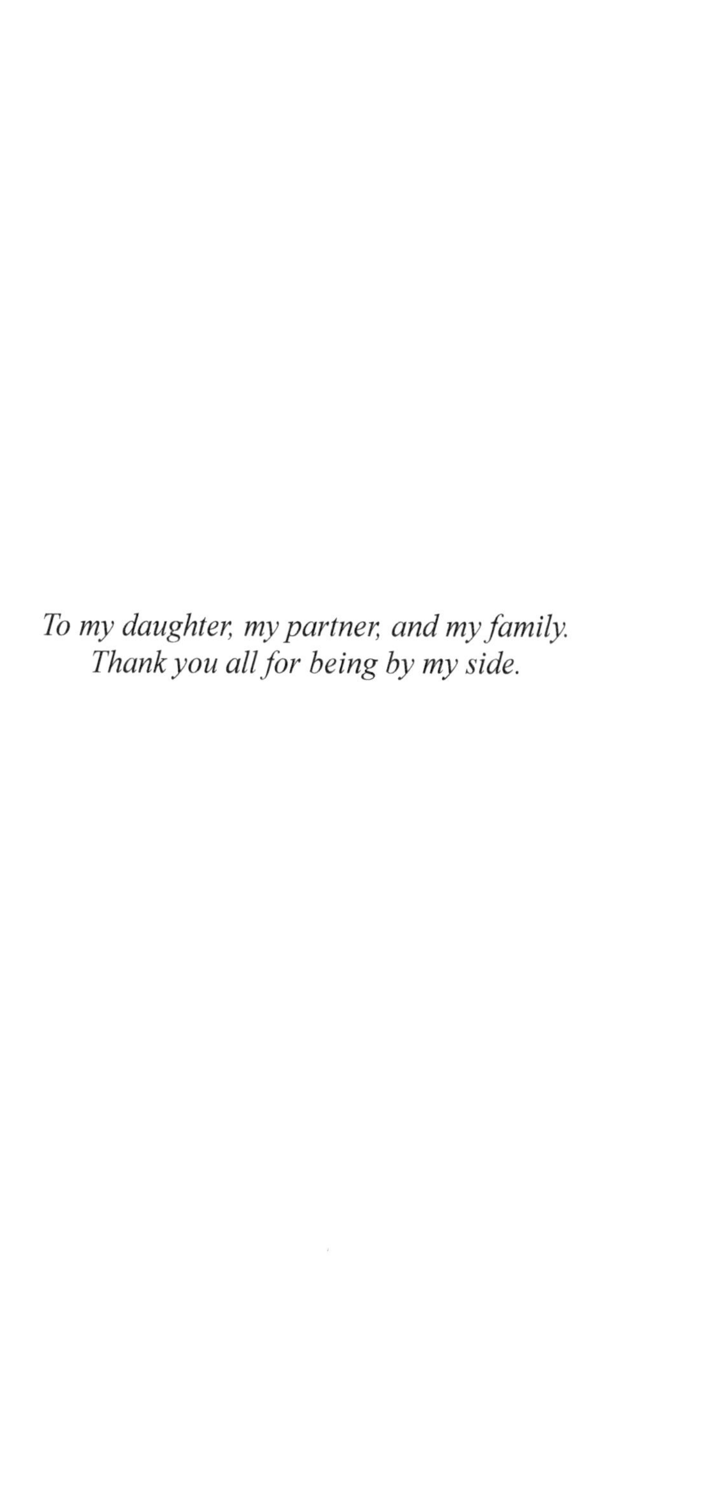

To my daughter, my partner, and my family.
Thank you all for being by my side.

Amaranthine

My love for you is amaranthine.
Our soul tied dream.
Your heart glows carmine.
My feelings are serene.
These tears are aquamarine.
Souls healed with codeine.
My love for you was amaranthine.

Love, xxx

Triple X like a dagger in my chest.
Search history.
Opposite of me.
Choke hold.
Cant breathe.
Help - That's not me.

Gentle.
Kind.
You make me feel safe.
Safety.
Safety.
Opposite of you.
Safety.
Safety.
Wait - that's not you.

Mama, Where?

1:44
Mama, where?
Shoved to my knees.
I'm begging please.
Mama, where?
Leave.
Left.
Mama, don't leave.

Broken Mirror

You are my mirror.
Our reflections in every fight.
Two souls holding on with all our might.
Two hearts trying to get through the night.

Divorce

5

A wild ray of light,
That runs blue,
Your white gown,
Mad with love,
Heartbreak awaits.

Love and Grief

I loved you through heavy storms of anger.
I loved you through the bitterness and the gentle.
I loved you through the cold, winter storms.
I loved you through the peaceful, calm summer
nights.
And because I have loved you, I have grieved.

My Anger Was Named Grief

Screaming.
Yelling.
Crying.
Slit Wrists.
Fight.
Long Nights.
No Sleep.
Angry.
Mad.
911.
Help.

Her name was grief.

Alone

Where do you go when the place you called
home, no longer feels familiar?
Who do you run to when the person who felt
like safety, no longer feels like comfort?
I want to go home.
Where is home?
You stole home, safety, familiarity, and comfort.
And now I am longing for a place of my own to
call home.

Single Parents

Breathe in.
Breathe out.
Get up.
You're all they have.

Love Yourself

Loving you was ice in my veins.
Loving you was rage and pain.
Loving you was laughter and grief.
Loving you was all that mattered.

Sober

Love is often compared to a drug.
Drugs are a monster and love is angelic.
How can they be so easily compared?
And then I met you.
You and love were both like drugs.
I craved you.
I needed you.
The bandaid of drugs ripped off.
You were the monster.

Love and Fire

You lit the flame of love in my heart.
You lifted my soul and made me whole.
You let my dreams fly into reality.
You held my hand and gave me hope.

But, me and you, are fire and gas.
We would burn this whole world down to save
each other.
And we'd still end up with scars.

My Daughter

You are gentle.
You are kind.
You're a strong superhero.
You're one of a kind.
You're passionate and your words hold weight.
You're brave.
You're my greatest gift.
You're my biggest blessing.

Why is heaven so far?

Another year has come and gone.
You're still too far away and I miss the old days.
The ache in my chest and I cannot rest.

People Change

Oh, how I loved you.
Oh, how you hurt me.
Oh, how I saved myself.
Oh, how you're out there broken.

Please, get help.

I tried to hide my demons.
They burned in my heart very much alive.
Get these voices out of my head.
Get these monsters out of my bed.
Help.
Help.
I made a deal with the devil.
The devil said his name was pain.

Verbal Abuse

Scream.
Run.
Hide.

Why can I not escape this shell that is holding
me?
I'm in a chokehold.

Scream.
Run.
Hide.

Why can I not break free from your hands
around my throat?
They told me it's just words, it shouldn't hurt.

Scream.
Run.
Cry.

Be Here For Both

Sometimes life is a beautiful blossom.
Sometimes life is so peaceful.
A fresh breeze on a warm day.

Sometimes life is a chaotic thunderstorm.
Sometimes life is a terrifying tornado.
A painful chill on a frigid day.